CELEB★★

FOOTBALL STAR

GEOFF BARKER

W

FRANKLIN WATTS

LONDON • SYDNEY

First published in 2010 by
Franklin Watts
338 Euston Road
London NW1 3BH

Franklin Watts Australia
Level 17/207 Kent Street
Sydney NSW 2000

ISBN: 978 0 7496 9265 0

Dewey classification number: 796.3'34'092

A CIP catalogue record for this book is available from the British Library.

Planning and production by Discovery Books Limited
Managing editor: Laura Durman
Editor: Clare Hibbert
Designer: D.R. ink
Picture research: Colleen Ruck

Printed in China

Franklin Watts is a division of Hachette Children's Books, an Hachette UK company.
www.hachette.co.uk

Photo acknowledgements: Getty Images: cover (Glyn Kirk/AFP), pp 4 (Mark Thompson),
6–7 (Odd Andersen/AFP), 7 (Paul Gilham), 8–9 (Alex Livesey), 13 (Alex Livesey), 14–15
(Alex Livesey), 16 (Antonio Scorza/AFP), 20 (Ross Kinnaird), 22 (Walter Astrada/AFP), 23
(Josep Lago/AFP), 25 (Paul Gilham), 28 (Jeff J. Mitchell), 29 (David Cannon); Rex Features:
pp 11 (Giuliano Bevilacqua), 12 (Simon Stacpoole), 17 (Action Press), 18, 21 (Rotello),
27 (Sipa Press); Shutterstock Images: pp 1 and 10 (Jonathan Larsen), 3 (Stawek), 5
(Sportsphotographer.eu), 19 and 31 (Alexander Gordeyev), 26 (Adam Gasson).

Every attempt has been made to clear copyright. Should there be any inadvertent omission,
please apply to the Publishers for rectification.

To the best of its knowledge, the Publisher believes the facts in this book to be true at the
time of going to press. However, due to the nature of celebrity, it is impossible to guarantee
that all the facts will still be current at the time of reading.

Note to parents and teachers:
Every effort has been made by
the Publishers to ensure that the
websites in this book are suitable
for children, that they are of the
highest educational value, and
that they contain no inappropriate
or offensive material. However,
because of the nature of the
Internet, it is impossible to
guarantee that the contents of
these sites will not be altered.
We strongly advise that Internet
access is supervised by
a responsible adult.

CONTENTS

fact

John Terry beat off fierce competition from Steven Gerrard and Rio Ferdinand to become England captain in 2008.

'I realise football's my life and I have got one chance at it.'

Terry in action during a qualifying match for the 2010 FIFA World Cup.

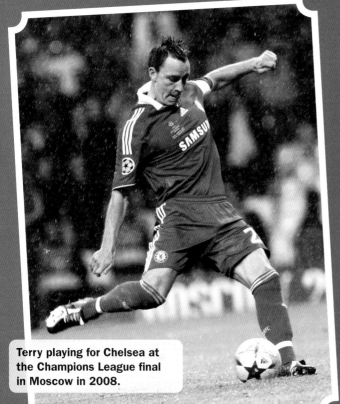

Terry playing for Chelsea at the Champions League final in Moscow in 2008.

CELEB BIO

Date of birth **7 December 1980**

Place of birth **Barking, Greater London, UK**

Position **Centre back**

Height **1.87m**

Biggest achievements **Chelsea captain in 2004–05 when Chelsea won Premiership; voted PFA Players' Player of the Year**

Training **Chelsea youth system from age 14**

Inspirational figures **Gianfranco Zola, Bobby Moore**

JOHN TERRY

Footballers are great athletes. Football is a very competitive sport, and only the very best stand a chance of making it. Top players like John Terry have to be tough, as well as talented.

WILL TO WIN

The best footballers, like John Terry, remain focused for the whole match. They love their club and play with passion, determined to win every game. Footballers also need to be disciplined and play by the rules. Being sent off for a foul lets down the whole team.

TEAM SPIRIT

Players have to pull together, work as a team and try to follow the manager's game plan. Strikers focus on attack, trying to score a goal in the opponents' net. Defenders try to cancel out the threat of the opposing team's strikers.

NO NONSENSE

Chelsea centre back John Terry is a no-nonsense defender. He reads the game well and makes brave challenges. He is brilliant in the air, either clearing the ball or scoring vital goals with his head from set pieces.

LEADER OF MEN

John Terry is mentally very strong. Thanks to his hard work and determination, he has authority on the pitch and in the dressing room. His teammates at Chelsea and England respect him. As captain of both club and country, he leads by example and motivates his players.

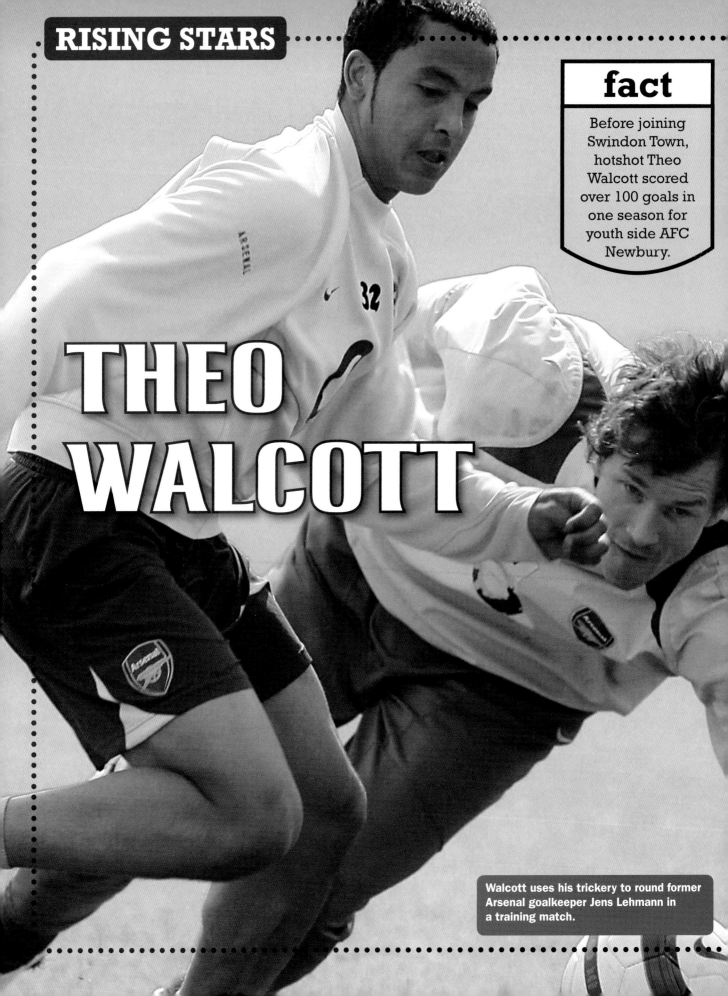

fact

Before joining Swindon Town, hotshot Theo Walcott scored over 100 goals in one season for youth side AFC Newbury.

THEO WALCOTT

Walcott uses his trickery to round former Arsenal goalkeeper Jens Lehmann in a training match.

A new generation of young players is emerging. Bright young stars like Theo Walcott develop their talents at training schemes set up by Premiership and League clubs – football academies and centres of excellence.

THROUGH THE RANKS

Most players join a local club's academy around the age of nine. At 16, a small handful of hopefuls are selected to carry on and join youth training schemes, which usually last three years – but most youngsters don't make it.

EARLY YEARS

Exceptional talents such as Theo Walcott shine as footballers at an early age. Walcott played at youth level for AFC Newbury, Swindon Town and Southampton. He broke into the Southampton first team in 2005 aged 16 and attracted the attention of the top clubs.

SIGNING FOR ARSENAL

Arsenal, which has a reputation for developing young talent, bought Walcott in 2006. Walcott has skill, trickery and raw pace. He uses these footballing qualities to outwit hardened professionals in a tough Premiership.

VERY BRIGHT FUTURE

Theo Walcott looks capable of becoming a great player. He is able to stay level-headed, even when he is playing a really crucial match. In only his second competitive start for England in 2008, he scored a memorable hat-trick against Croatia in an important 2010 World Cup qualifying game.

Walcott looks on during a UEFA Under-21 Championship qualifying match between Portugal and England.

CELEB BIO

Date of birth
16 March 1989
Place of birth
Stanmore, Greater London, UK
Position **Winger**
Height **1.75m**
Biggest achievement **Being picked for the 2006 World Cup squad; becoming the youngest player to score a hat-trick for England (in 2008)**
Training **Swindon Town and Southampton youth teams**
Inspirational figures **Robbie Fowler, Michael Owen, Thierry Henry**

'I have been around for quite a long time... but I am still learning my trade.'

STEVEN GERRARD

The club manager picks the team and sets out a game plan. But during the match, it is the team captain who leads the players on the pitch. The captain tries to motivate his players to play at their very best.

LEADING BY EXAMPLE

Football captains are leaders. They help to make 11 individuals play together as a team. They must lead by example, showing energy and drive on the pitch. As club captain, Steven Gerrard is the heart and soul of Liverpool's side.

PRODUCT OF YOUTH TRAINING

Local lad Gerrard joined Liverpool's youth academy when he was nine. He made his debut for Liverpool FC at the age of 18 in 1998. Liverpool saw that the skinny young midfielder had leadership qualities. In 2003 he replaced Sami Hyypia as club captain.

DRIVING FORCE

Although Gerrard felt out of his depth playing in his first season, he quickly settled. As he grew stronger, he became a fierce tackler. Gerrard developed a dynamic playing style, dominating the midfield and driving on his team. He also contributes vital goals during a season, many of them blasted in from outside the box.

FIGHTING BACK

Liverpool have an inspirational captain in Gerrard. In the 2005 Champions League final, the team was 3–0 down at half-time against AC Milan. Gerrard scored with a header to lead an incredible fightback. Within six minutes, the score was 3–3! Liverpool won on penalties and Gerrard, as captain, lifted the Champions League trophy. It was an unforgettable moment.

'I've got absolutely no intention of ever going to play at another club.'

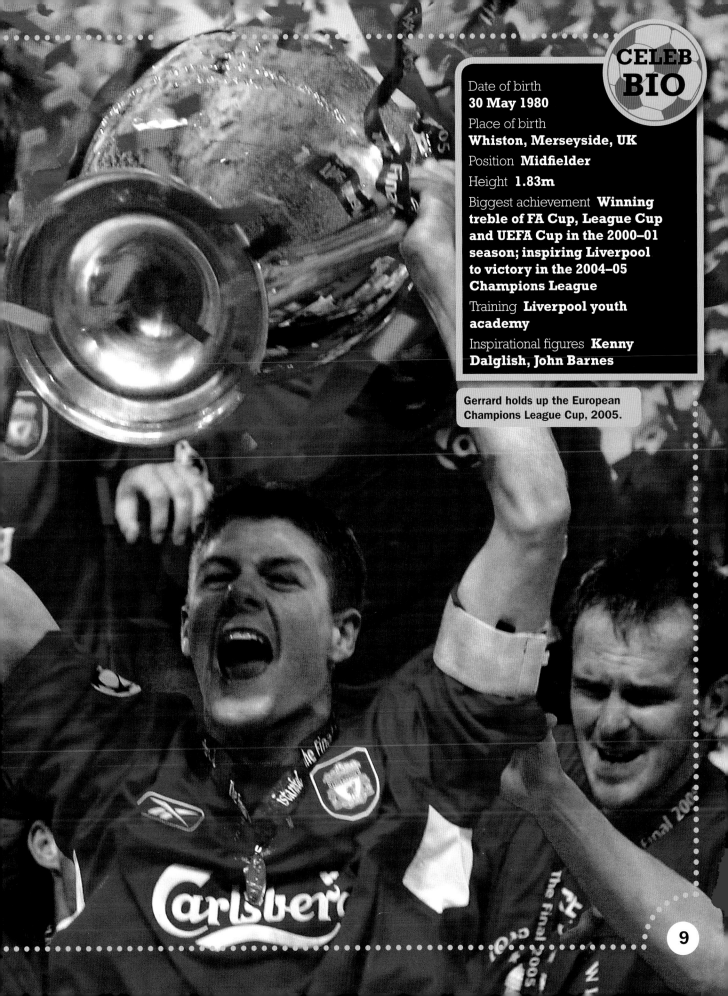

Date of birth
30 May 1980

Place of birth
Whiston, Merseyside, UK

Position **Midfielder**

Height **1.83m**

Biggest achievement **Winning treble of FA Cup, League Cup and UEFA Cup in the 2000–01 season; inspiring Liverpool to victory in the 2004–05 Champions League**

Training **Liverpool youth academy**

Inspirational figures **Kenny Dalglish, John Barnes**

Gerrard holds up the European Champions League Cup, 2005.

CRISTIANO RONALDO

Premiership football is all about power and pace. Fans also love to see skilful players like Cristiano Ronaldo showing their special tricks and flicks – as long as they work. Slip up and the side can go a goal down.

Ronaldo in action for Portugal in a UEFA Euro 2008 quarter-final match against Germany.

TRICKY CUSTOMERS

Footballers spend hours training hard with the squad. The most gifted players also use their time on the training ground to work out and practise new tricks. Back flicks and step-overs are great to watch at a game. Managers insist that players come up with an 'end product', though – a goal or an assist for a goal.

NOT A 'SHOW PONY'

Cristiano Ronaldo joined Manchester United in 2003, signing for £12.2 million. He wore the famous number 7 shirt, once filled by legends such as George Best, Eric Cantona and David Beckham. Young Ronaldo was accused of showing off with all his skills and flicks, but he quickly adapted his game to England's tough Premiership and won over his critics.

£80-MILLION MAN

Ronaldo's 2007–08 season ended with a massive haul of 42 goals in total. A master of practice and technique, he has perfected free kicks from just outside the box. The dazzling winger continues to beat players with a bewildering range of tricks. In 2009 he joined Spanish club Real Madrid, for a record-breaking transfer fee of £80 million.

CELEB BIO

Date of birth
5 February 1985

Place of birth
Funchal, Madeira, Portugal

Position **Winger**

Height **1.85m**

Biggest achievement **Winning the 2007–08 Champions League with Man Utd; being named Man of the Match in the final against Chelsea**

Training **Sporting Lisbon football academy**

Inspirational figure **Diego Maradona**

'I believe I can win [World Player of the Year] again.'

FERNANDO TORRES

fact

At the beginning of the 2009–10 season, more than half the Premiership players were foreign-born (347 players out of 595).

Torres scores a header for Liverpool in a league match against Blackburn Rovers.

Some footballers find it difficult playing for a foreign team. Players like Liverpool's Fernando Torres have to adapt to living abroad and starting at a new club, where everything is different. Some never quite settle and have to move on again.

OVERSEAS TALENT

Talented new players can boost a squad. Just 22 overseas players featured during the first season of the Premier League in 1992–93, but over the years, more and more foreign players have graced the English Premiership with their skills, including Italian Gianfranco Zola, German Michael Ballack, Frenchman Thierry Henry and Brazilian Robinho. The influx of foreign footballers can improve the overall quality of play in a league.

TEAM SUPPORT

Classy Spanish striker Fernando Torres joined Liverpool from Atlético Madrid in 2007. With a Spanish manager and fellow Spaniard Pepe Reina in goal, Torres settled quickly. His teammates and the fans supported him. Even so, on the pitch he had to adapt to a much more physical game than he was used to.

GRIT AND DETERMINATION

Torres relished the challenge. He has pace, guts and the will to win. A brilliant and cool finisher for club and country, he makes scoring goals look easy. In his first two seasons at Liverpool, Torres scored 50 goals.

PLAYING FOR SPAIN

Torres made his debut for Spain in 2003 against Portugal. He has since become a key player for his country, taking part in Euro 2004 and 2008, and the 2006 World Cup. He scored three goals in the World Cup finals and clinched Euro 2008 by scoring the winning goal in the final against Germany.

CELEB BIO

Date of birth **20 March 1984**
Place of birth **Madrid, Spain**
Position **Striker**
Height **1.86m**
Biggest achievement **Scoring the only goal in the Euro 2008 final for Spain against Germany**
Training **Atlético Madrid junior teams since age 11**
Inspirational figures **Ex-Atlético Madrid player Kiko, basketball player Michael Jordan, cyclist Miguel Indurain**

Torres waves his national flag after scoring for Spain in the Euro 2008 final against Germany.

'Upon arriving at a new place you must want to learn and also be ready to listen to advice.'

WAYNE ROONEY

Playing for a top club is exciting, especially for the lucky footballers who end up playing for a club they've supported since boyhood. Playing for your country, though, is the greatest honour of all.

CLUB VS COUNTRY

Many good club players never get picked for the national side. Others may not shine when playing for their country. It's not just about playing well in big competitions such as the UEFA European Football Championship and the World Cup. Footballers have to impress in friendlies as well.

BOY WONDER

At just 16, Wayne Rooney burst on to the football scene. Playing for Everton, he scored a breathtaking, curling match-winner against Arsenal to become the youngest goalscorer in Premier League history. England had a new star in the making.

ENGLAND REGULAR

With the spotlight on him, Rooney developed into a regular in the England team. An exciting footballer with great strength and determination, he has proved a hit with England fans. Rooney was injured before the 2006 World Cup and his weak performance contributed to England's early exit from the tournament. Two years later, England failed to qualify for Euro 2008. This disappointment drives Rooney on.

STRENGTH TO STRENGTH

Rooney is an explosive, physical presence on a football pitch. Developing his skills with Manchester United, he will get even better. He has already set his sights on breaking another United legend's record – Bobby Charlton's 49 goals for England.

CELEB BIO

Date of birth **24 October 1985**

Place of birth **Croxteth, Liverpool, UK**

Position **Striker**

Height **1.78m**

Claim to fame **Becoming youngest footballer to play for England at 17 in 2003 (Theo Walcott has since broken this record)**

Biggest achievement **Winning both the Premiership and the Champions League in 2007–08 with Man Utd**

Training **Everton Academy from age 10**

Inspirational figures **Former Everton player Duncan Ferguson, United teammates Ryan Giggs and Paul Scholes**

England's Rooney shoots during a 2010 World Cup qualifying match against Belarus.

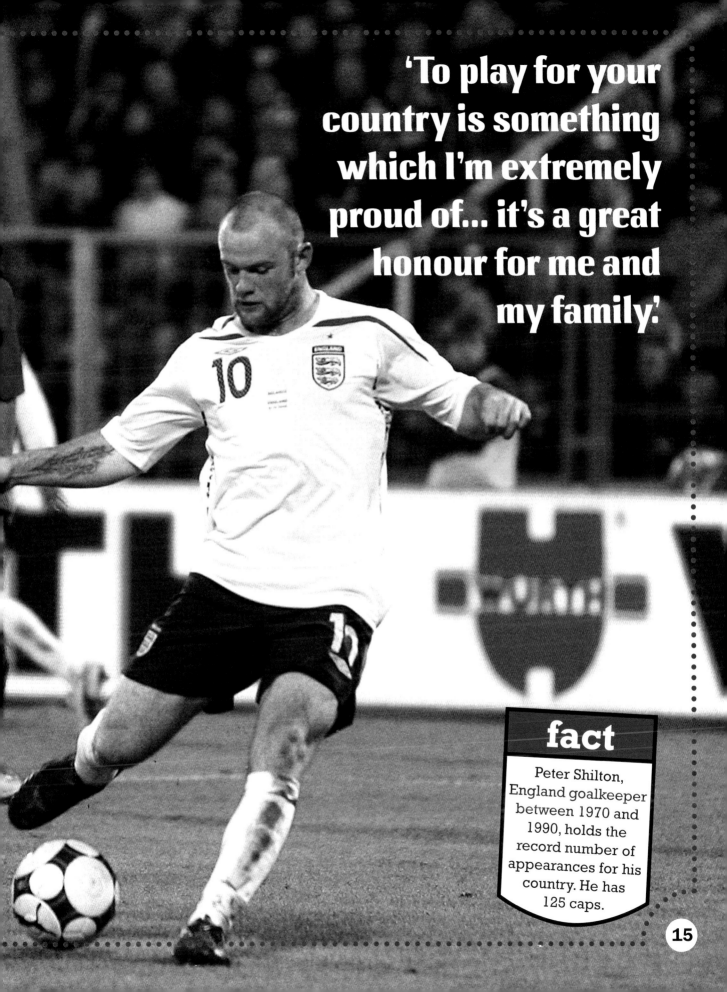

'To play for your country is something which I'm extremely proud of... it's a great honour for me and my family.'

fact

Peter Shilton, England goalkeeper between 1970 and 1990, holds the record number of appearances for his country. He has 125 caps.

RONALDO

The FIFA World Cup is football's ultimate prize. Nations play qualifying matches to earn the right to compete every four years. The 2006 World Cup final between Italy and France was watched by 715 million people.

WORLD CUP FINALS

Every four years, a different country is chosen to host the World Cup. Over a period of a month, 32 national teams play in eight different groups, followed by dramatic knockout games. After three games each, the top two sides from each group go forward. Teams then play each other to reach the quarter-finals, semi-finals and final.

O FENOMENO

Ronaldo – short for Ronaldo Luís Nazário de Lima – is a World Cup hero. Like fellow-Brazilian superstar Pelé, he travelled to his first World Cup finals aged 17. And, like Pelé, he returned home with the trophy. Nicknamed *O Fenomeno* ('The Phenomenon'), Ronaldo terrorised opposition defences with his pace and strength. The striker also helped Brazil win the World Cup in 2002.

COMEBACK KID

Ronaldo had a setback in the 1998 World Cup. He could not cope with the pressure of being the team's star and played poorly – Brazil lost the final 3–0 to France. Despite this blow and serious injuries in 1999 and 2000, Ronaldo bounced back for the 2002 World Cup. He was top scorer with eight goals.

Brazilian fans support Ronaldo at the 2002 World Cup in Japan.

'The best player I ever worked with? It has to be Brazil's Ronaldo... lean, mean and quick as an Olympic sprinter.'
FORMER ENGLAND MANAGER, BOBBY ROBSON

CELEB BIO

Date of birth
22 September 1976

Place of birth
Rio de Janeiro, Brazil

Position **Striker**

Height **1.83m**

Claim to fame **Aged only 16, scoring 12 goals in 14 games for Brazilian club side Cruzeiro in his first season**

Biggest achievement **Becoming the highest goalscorer in the history of the World Cup with a record-breaking 15th goal in 2006**

Training **Sao Cristovao and other local Rio de Janeiro youth teams**

Inspirational figures **Brazil team from 1982 World Cup, including Falcao, Socrates and Zico**

Ronaldo holds high the World Cup in 2002.

DAVID BECKHAM

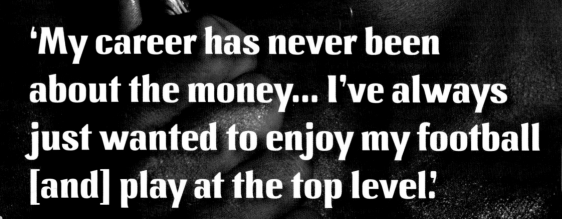

'My career has never been about the money... I've always just wanted to enjoy my football [and] play at the top level.'

Beckham appears in an advert for a new razor.

What have top English players John Terry, Frank Lampard, Steven Gerrard and Wayne Rooney got in common? They all earn six-figure salaries. That's over £100,000 – every week! But one player is richer than all of them... David Beckham.

Beckham playing for England against Kazakhstan in a qualifying match for the 2010 World Cup.

MAKING MONEY

Football is big money. Football clubs may spend vast sums on certain players, but they make their money back by selling match tickets and club merchandise, and through deals to televise their games. They also receive sponsorship from big companies that pay to have their names on players' shirts or to advertise at football grounds.

FAMOUS ICON

Global superstar David Beckham, or 'Becks', is more famous than any other sportsperson. He began his footballing career at Manchester United when he was a still a teenager. During his 10 years there, he married pop star 'Posh Spice' (Victoria Adams of the Spice Girls), was made captain of the English side and was twice runner-up for FIFA World Player of the Year. Thanks to his talent and good looks, he became a sporting icon.

DRESS SENSE... AND BUSINESS SENSE

As a stylish, fashionable man, Beckham has become a well-known 'brand'. He makes lots of money by advertising sports names such as Adidas. He also models clothes, sunglasses and wristwatches. David Beckham topped football's 'rich list' in 2009 with a fortune of £145 million. His most successful playing days may be behind him, but Becks is still a star.

CELEB BIO

Date of birth **2 May 1975**

Place of birth **Leytonstone, Greater London, UK**

Position **Midfielder**

Height **1.83m**

Biggest achievement **Winning a unique treble of Premier League, FA Cup and Champions League in 1998–99 with Man Utd**

Training **Signed schoolboy forms for Man Utd aged 14; youth training scheme contract aged 16**

Inspirational figures **Bryan Robson, Nelson Mandela, Muhammad Ali**

ASHLEY & CHERYL COLE

Top footballers are appreciated for their skills on the pitch. These days, many of the most famous footballers are also known for their beautiful companions – 'Wives And Girlfriends', or WAGs for short.

A DISTRACTION?

In 2006, England stumbled out of the World Cup at the quarter-final stage. Some blamed the glamorous WAGs who accompanied the team to Germany and spent their time partying and shopping. During the 2010 World Cup qualifying stages, England manager Fabio Capello told the WAGs to stay at home so that the players could concentrate on their game.

PERFECT COUPLE

Ashley Cole plays left back for Chelsea and England. Before Chelsea, he spent six seasons at Arsenal and collected several honours, including two League medals. In 2006 Cole married Cheryl Tweedy, singer in the band Girls Aloud.

A SUCCESSFUL WOMAN

Cheryl Cole had a very successful singing career before dating and marrying a famous footballer. In 2008, she replaced Sharon Osbourne as an *X Factor* judge, becoming even more of a celebrity, and often outshining her sporting husband.

'CASHLEY' COLE

Despite his footballing successes, Ashley Cole is not as popular as his wife. In 2006 he annoyed Arsenal fans by moving to London rivals Chelsea and was also criticised for moaning about Arsenal in his autobiography. He became famous for complaining about earning only £55,000 a week – and gained the nickname 'Cashley' Cole.

Cheryl Tweedy (now Cole), Colleen McLoughlin (now Rooney) and Victoria Beckham at the 2006 World Cup.

'[Most WAGs] have nannies, they don't cook or clean and never do a day's work.' CHERYL COLE

The Coles at Cheryl's 26th birthday party.

CELEB BIO

Name **Ashley Cole**

Date of birth **20 December 1980**

Place of birth **Stepney, London, UK**

Position **Left back**

Height **1.73m**

Claim to fame **Winning the Premiership and FA Cup double with Arsenal in 2001–02**

Biggest achievement **Winning five FA Cup medals (with Arsenal in 2002, 2003 and 2005 and with Chelsea in 2007 and 2009)**

Training **Arsenal youth system**

Inspirational figures **Former Arsenal player David Rocastle**

fact

Cheryl Cole got a 50 per cent pay rise as judge in the fifth series of *The X Factor*... to £1.2 million!

21

SAMUEL ETO'O

Eto'o in the Ugandan capital, Kampala, running a football clinic for local schoolchildren.

fact

Samuel Eto'o has scored more goals in the history of the African Nations Cup than any other player.

Today, some footballers are more like pop idols than sports players. We see them on the TV and read a lot about them, but do footballers make good role models? Cameroon international Samuel Eto'o certainly does!

Eto'o playing for Barcelona.

ON AND OFF THE PITCH

Sometimes footballers behave badly on the pitch. Some dive to get a free kick or a vital penalty, push the referee or even start fights. Off the pitch, many footballers have gone clubbing, got drunk and got into trouble. Some have crashed their top-of-the-range sports cars.

DOING GOOD

Playing football at the highest level brings great wealth and success. This can go to some players' heads. Others, like Samuel Eto'o, use their unique position to promote worthwhile causes and charities. Eto'o is a world-class striker. In his first five seasons with Barcelona he scored more than 100 goals.

MAKING A STAND

Eto'o campaigns against racism in football. He once threatened to walk off during a match after abuse from fans. He argues that no one should feel 'looked down upon because of the colour of their skin'. He also believes strongly in doing charity work. He has donated ambulances, set up football academies and helped schools in several African countries.

CELEB BIO

Date of birth
10 March 1981

Place of birth
Douala, Cameroon

Position **Striker**

Height **1.80m**

Claim to fame **Playing for Cameroon against Costa Rica in 1996 aged only 14**

Biggest achievement **Scoring for Barcelona in two Champions League finals – in 2006 against Arsenal and in 2009 against Man Utd**

Training **Real Madrid youth system**

Inspirational figure **Roger Milla, Cameroon striker and star of the 1990 World Cup**

'Having millions of people watch you play and be influenced by what you do is a huge responsibility. I consider it to be a great honour.'

RYAN GIGGS

Football clubs would be nothing without their supporters. Fans follow their team through thick and thin, and most supporters have a favourite player. Footballers like Ryan Giggs, who play for the same side for years, have a special relationship with their fans.

DEVOTED FANS

Many football fans have a season ticket for their favourite team. They wear replica football shirts. Some help write club fanzines or they blog football fansites and websites with news and views on players and matches.

LIFTING THE TEAM

Fans will try to lift their team. Premiership matches are famous for their passion, energy and noise. Silent, empty stadiums suddenly fill on match days, tense with excitement. A deafening roar erupts when a player scores – and fans chant his name.

ONE-CLUB HERO

Welsh wizard Ryan Giggs is loved by his army of fans. He joined Manchester United as a youngster and since then has made over 800 appearances for the team. He also plays for Wales. It is rare that a good player stays with one club. Successful players usually move from club to club in pursuit of greater success and higher wages.

THE RIGHT DECISION

Giggs's loyalty has been rewarded by winning heaps of honours with England's top club – including 10 Premiership titles and the Champions League in 1999 and 2008. For Manchester United fans, this one-club hero is a living legend.

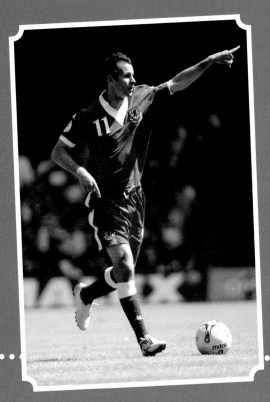

'I had a great reception from the crowd and that gives you an extra lift, an extra buzz.'

Giggs playing his last game for Wales in 2007.

CELEB BIO

Date of birth
29 November 1973

Place of birth
Cardiff, Wales, UK

Position **Winger**

Height **1.80m**

Claim to fame **Becoming PFA Young Player of the Year 1992 in his first full season – and repeating the feat in 1993**

Biggest achievement **Winning the treble in 1998–99 (see page 19); being BBC Sports Personality 2009**

Training **Manchester City School of Excellence, then Man Utd apprenticeship**

Inspirational figures **Bryan Robson and Nelson Mandela**

'I know nothing about tactics. I just get good players on the pitch who can run a bit.'

GORDON STRACHAN

fact

Strachan is famous for his jokey post-match interviews. Here's just one:

REPORTER: So, Gordon, in what areas do you think Middlesbrough were better than you today?

STRACHAN: What areas? Mainly that big green one out there…

Strachan shouts instructions to Celtic during a Champions League match in 2007.

Is there life after a successful playing career? Most footballers have a fairly short career of 10 to 15 years. But how can they get the same sort of excitement – the highs and the lows – from another job?

STAYING IN FOOTBALL

Most ex-footballers wish to continue with the game in some way. Some offer their knowledge and expert opinion to the media. Ex-footballers write newspaper columns and become pundits on the TV and radio.

MANAGING

Many ex-players decide to become football managers. Clubs compete for just a few trophies each year, so management is stressful. First a manager needs to train and qualify as a coach. Then he needs to succeed... quickly.

PLAYING CAREER

Gordon Strachan played for Aberdeen, Manchester United and Leeds United. He made over 600 club appearances and also won 50 caps for Scotland. At the age of 35, as captain of Leeds, the fiery right-sided midfielder won the 1992 Championship.

MOVING INTO MANAGEMENT

Strachan first managed Coventry before joining Southampton. In 2003, the 'Saints' lost to Arsenal in the FA Cup final, but qualified for Europe. In 2004, Strachan left management to spend more time with his family. He worked on TV as a popular football pundit, alongside Adrian Chiles on *Match of the Day 2*. In 2005, Strachan became manager of Celtic. He guided them to three Scottish Premier League titles in a row. He left Celtic after rivals Rangers won the 2008–09 title, later becoming manager at Middlesbrough.

Strachan playing for Scotland in a FIFA World Cup 1986 qualifying match against Spain.

CELEB BIO

Date of birth
9 February 1957

Place of birth
Edinburgh, Scotland, UK

Position **Midfielder**

Height **1.68m**

Claim to fame **Winning the European Cup Winners' Cup in 1983 with Aberdeen**

Biggest achievement **The only player to win FWA Footballer of the Year on both sides of the English-Scottish border**

Inspirational figures **Tommy Burns, Kenny Dalglish, Graeme Souness**

GLOSSARY

abuse Bad treatment by someone.

AFC Short for Amateur Football Club.

apprenticeship Learning a job or trade from a skilled employer.

assist Pass or cross to a player who then scores.

back flick A move where the footballer passes the ball using the heel of his or her foot.

brand A recognized product or range of products, or a celebrity who puts his or her name to products.

campaign To systematically fight towards achieving a particular aim.

cap Each appearance a player makes for the national team.

centre of excellence A special training school.

debut First appearance or game.

defender A player who is positioned to defend the goal and goalkeeper. Defence usually consists of a left back, right back and two centre backs.

discipline Strict rules for behaviour.

dribbling Using close ball control to run past another team's players.

dynamic Bursting with energy.

fanzine Fan magazine.

FC Short for Football Club.

FIFA Short for *Fédération Internationale de Football Association*. The organization that runs international football and that is in charge of the FIFA World Cup.

football academy A school or college that provides football training for young people.

friendly A game that is not a competitive cup or league match.

FWA Short for Football Writers' Association.

hat-trick (1) When a player scores three goals in a single match. (2) Three wins in a row.

icon Symbol or image.

influx The arrival of many people or things.

inspirational Able to urge others on to do special things.

media The ways to communicate news, such as TV, newspapers and websites.

midfielder A player who is positioned in the middle of the pitch, as a link between the attackers and defenders. Most teams play a left, centre and right midfield.

motivate To urge on.

PFA Short for Professional Footballers' Association.

professional Someone who does a particular, skilled job for a living.

pundits Experts.

racism Discrimination against or abuse of people because of their race.

replica shirt A mass-produced sports top that looks just like a player's shirt.

role model Someone who sets a good example to others.

schoolboy forms Agreements signed by youngsters aged between nine and 16 to train and play for a football club at junior level. The forms are renewed every year or every two years, if the club is happy with the young player's progress.

set piece A free kick or a corner.

squad All of a club's players, not just the team.

step-over A move where the footballer steps over the ball while dribbling in order to trick an opponent and change direction.

striker An attacker who plays in front of the midfield and is responsible for scoring goals.

UEFA Short for Union of European Football Clubs. The organization that runs European football and that is in charge of the UEFA European Football Championship, the UEFA Champions League and the UEFA Cup.

winger An attacking midfielder or striker, who usually pushes forwards down one flank (and is therefore named a left or a right winger) in order to broaden the attack.

youth training scheme A placement for a young person that allows them to receive training on the job.

FURTHER INFORMATION

BOOKS

21st Century Lives: Footballers by Liz Gogerly (Wayland, 2007)

21st Century Lives: World Cup Footballers by Adam Sutherland (Wayland, 2010)

Dream to Win: David Beckham by Roy Apps (Franklin Watts, 2010)

Dream to Win: Wayne Rooney by Roy Apps (Franklin Watts, 2008)

Fantastic Football by Clive Gifford (OUP, 2010)

Football Academy: Boys United by Tom Palmer (Puffin, 2009)

Football Encyclopedia by Clive Gifford (Kingfisher, 2006)

Football Focus: Players and Skills by Clive Gifford (Wayland, 2009)

Football Mad by John Goodwin, Alan MacDonald and Helena Pielichaty (OUP, 2008)

Goal!: Cup Final Day by David James (Ransom Publishing, 2008)

Top Trumps: World Football Stars 2 by Tim Dykes and Nick Judd (J H Haynes and Co Ltd, 2008)

Training to Succeed: Football by Edward Way (Franklin Watts, 2009)

DVDS

Boys from Brazil, presented by John Motson (2 Entertain, 2006)

FIFA Fever – Best of the FIFA World Cup (Go Entertain, 2006)

History of Football, presented by Alan Green (Go Entertain, 2006)

WEBSITES

http://news.bbc.co.uk/sport1/hi/football/
Latest news, results, fixtures, tables and football from all around the world. Plus transfer gossip.

http://www.metro.co.uk/football
Up-to-date news and views in newspaper sports page format.

http://www.goal.com/en
Football website packed with interesting football news and information.

www.fifa.com/worldcup/index.html
The official website of the FIFA World Cup.

http://uk.eurosport.yahoo.com/07082009/58/top-50-players-1-lionel-messi.html
List of best players in the world.